LAUREL & HARDY

Quote Unquote

LAUREL & HARDY

 QUOTE UNQUOTE

Neil Grant

CRESCENT BOOKS
NEW YORK • AVENEL

AUTHOR'S NOTE

Everyone who writes about Laurel and Hardy owes a great debt to the American actor and scholar John McCabe, who wrote four books about them. His long talks with Stan in his latter years provide many of the quotes in this book.

PICTURE CREDITS

British Film Institute pages 9, 30, 36, 37, 40, 41, 42, 43, 45, 53, 54, 56, 77; **Ronald Grant Archive** front cover, opener, pages 10, 11, 13, 14, 17, 18, 22, 26, 31, 44, 46, 51, 52, 59, 60, 63, 64, 71 (right), 72, 74, 75; **Hulton Deutsch Collection** pages 6, 24, 71 (left), 76, 78; **Pictorial Press** back cover, pages 25, 66, 68, 69, 70; **Range/Bettman/UPI** page 19; **Rex Features** page 62.

This 1995 edition published by
Crescent Books, distributed by Random House Value
Publishing, Inc.,
40 Englehard Avenue, Avenel, New Jersey 07001.

Random House
New York • Toronto • London • Sydney • Auckland

A CIP catalog record for this book is available from the
Library of Congress

Copyright © 1994 Parragon Book Service Ltd
All rights reserved

Publishing Manager: Sally Harper
Editor: Barbara Horn
Design and DTP: Crump Design

ISBN 1 85813 841 8

Printed in Italy

CONTENTS

INNOCENT ANARCHISTS

'[Babe] was like a brother to me. We seemed to sense each other. Funny, we never really got to know each other personally until we took the tours together. When we made pictures it was all business even though it was fun. Between pictures we hardly saw each other. His life outside the studio was sports — and my life was practically all work, even after work was over. I loved editing and cutting the pictures, something he wasn't interested in. But whatever I did was tops with him. There was never any argument between us, never.'

'In Florida, when I was working for Lubin [film studio], we used to get our hair cut at an Italian barber's who had a shop right near our studio. He had a thick foreign accent and he was also a boy who liked boys. Well, he took a great fancy to me and every time after he'd finish shaving me, he'd rub powder into my face and pat my cheeks and say, "Nice-a bab-ee. Nice-a bab-ee". The gang always used to kid me about it and after a while they started to call me "Baby" and then it was cut down to "Babe".'

HOW MR HARDY BECAME 'BABE'

'I have never really worked hard in the creation department. After all, just doing the gags is hard enough work, especially if you've taken as many falls and been dumped in as many mudholes as I have. I think I've earned my money.'

HOW BABE EARNED HIS KEEP

TOGETHER, Stan Laurel and Oliver Hardy belonged to an old tradition, springing from the music hall, of the two-man comedy team. Unusually, there was no real straight man, though Hardy was always the 'fall guy', the one who ended up sitting in the goldfish pond.

The Laurel and Hardy on-screen characters were known as Stan and Ollie. In real life, Stan was still Stan, but 'Ollie', as Hardy is called in the films, was known to his friends as 'Babe'.

They were an incredibly prolific partnership. The exact number of films they made individually — one- or two-reelers lasting ten or twenty minutes — is uncertain, but as a team they made over one hundred. They stuck together from the late 1920s until Hardy's death in 1957. And they stayed partners that long not just because that was the only way they could make a living, but because, unusually, they were good friends too. Although Stan could be temperamental, he and Babe never seem to have had a serious disagreement. Hardy was as genial as fat men are reputed to be but seldom are.

Hardy was essentially an actor, keen only to do a good job, take his salary cheque and hotfoot it for the golf course. But for Stanley, comedy was his life, and when shooting ended for the day, he kept on working. Laurel was never named as director or scriptwriter, but his creative input was almost as great as Chaplin's was on his films. It was not until the Stan and Ollie revival of the 1950s that Stan began to be seen as a creator of film comedy who could stand on the same stage as Charlie Chaplin, Buster Keaton, Harry Langdon and earlier greats like Dan Leno.

In 1932, after seven years of continual work, Stan and Babe ventured out of the little world of Hollywood. They had been working so hard the previous five years that they had scarcely left it. They needed a holiday, and they decided to take it abroad, in Stan's native Britain. They got as far as Chicago before they were engulfed. News of their movements had spread, and everywhere fans had turned out in vast numbers, together with other hangers-on of the famous: journalists eager for interviews, cameramen working for newsreels, policemen striving to keep the masses under control. It was just as bad in New York, and even worse in Europe, where they were especially popular.

Stan and Babe were flabbergasted. They had hardly grasped the fact that in the past few years they had become worldwide stars,

'Like everybody else, I was interested in making money. This stems from my vaudeville days, when I was making very little of it.' STAN ON MONEY

LEFT: *Stan Laurel in costume for A-Haunting We Will Go (1942).*

and the media being less ubiquitous in those days, public attention on such a scale was completely unexpected. Their journey turned into a triumphal progress, though often a chaotic one. They were more tired out than refreshed by the time they got back to Los Angeles, with Babe lamenting that he had not been able to play one round of golf on the famous Scottish links that had lured him across the Atlantic in the first place.

They were then at their peak. In fact, if one agrees with the preponderant opinion that their finest films were the two- and three-reelers of the late 1920s and early 1930s, they were soon to start downhill. Henceforth they concentrated on features. The only trouble with most of their feature films of the 1930s is that they are a bit boring when Stan and Ollie are off the screen.

'A friend once asked me what comedy was. That floored me. What is comedy? I don't know. Does anybody? Can you define it? All I know is that I learned how to get laughs, and that's all I know about it.' STAN ON COMEDY

RIGHT: *Oliver Hardy in
A-Haunting We Will Go.*

It wasn't until they were taken over by
Fox in the 1940s that the rot really set in.
Fox treated them like second-rate contract
players and refused to allow Stan any artistic
input. Laurel and Hardy made the films for
Fox purely and simply for the money – and
hated them. Stan, who, in general, enjoyed
a comparatively serene, though not wealthy,
old age, never forgave the Fox studio bosses
for their insensitive treatment.

Laurel and Hardy had one professional
ambition, and only one: they wanted to
make people laugh. They laboured under no
false illusions about themselves. Their meth-
ods were those of the clown, and their
humour was the 'low' humour of the gag-
ster. Not much subtlety or pathos was called
upon, although that does not mean it was
entirely absent. But they did not court the
resonances of a Buster Keaton or a Charlie
Chaplin, whom they acknowledged as a
superior artist.

Certainly, the screen characters of Stan
and Ollie, were no intellectuals! In fact,
they were – and this was the basis of their
comedy – incredibly stupid. As Ollie once
remarked, they reason they appealed so
much to children was that any eight-year-
old could feel immeasurably more intelligent than they. Superficially, Stan was the

dumbest. At any rate he did the dumbest things – like telling Ollie on the phone that he had been bitten by a dog, and in reply to the question 'Where?', applying the phone to the injured part as if Ollie could see down the line. Stan was plain daft. But, to quote Ollie again, Ollie was really the dumbest, because he was the one who thought he was smart!

'There is no one as dumb as a dumb guy who thinks he's smart.' BABE ON OLLIE

Perhaps a more fundamental feature of their comedy is their innocence, and this may be the secret of their appeal to children, for they are like children themselves. Though they often have screen wives, these ladies usually appear more as authority figures – usually of some malignity – to be dodged or appeased. There is plenty of old-fashioned vulgarity, but no sexual innuendo. Stan and Ollie generally seem to sleep in the same bed, but no one has dared to suggest homosexual undertones.

A few of Laurel and Hardy's films, or passages from them, are surely as funny as anything in cinema. On the other hand, in such a large oeuvre there are plenty of duds. Some people, women more often than men, are immune to their humour; such people are usually immune to all forms of slapstick. These critics say that Laurel and Hardy are crude and that they are repetitive, using the same idiosyncratic tricks or gestures in every film.

This is all perfectly true. It also misses the point. Those criticisms could be made of all the great clowns. A custard pie thrown in someone's face is certainly crude; it also is, or can be, funny. Laurel and Hardy were not about art, and they were not particularly interested in plot. Ollie doing that little fiddle with his necktie is not especially funny in itself; it's much funnier when you're half waiting for it. A man falling off the roof into a pond may be only moderately funny the first time you see it. When it happens five times, and is carefully handled so that on the fifth occasion you see only the vacant roofline and a split second later hear the splash, the cumulative effect can be devastating to the ribs.

'I was expecting it [a bucket of water full in the face during WHY GIRLS LOVE SAILORS, 1927], and yet, in a way, I wasn't. … It threw me mentally, just for a second or so, and I just couldn't think of what to do next. The camera was grinding away, and I knew I had to do SOMETHING, so I thought of blowing my nose with my wet and sopping tie. I was raising my tie to my nose when all of a sudden I realized that this would be a bit vulgar. There were some ladies watching us. So I waved the tie in a kind of tiddly-widdly fashion, in a kind of comic way, to show that I was embarrassed.'

HOW OLLIE FIRST TWIDDLED HIS TIE

RIGHT: *Stan and Ollie built up a series of comic tricks and gestures throughout their films — including Ollie's distinctive tie-twiddle.*

YOUNG STAN

---

*'The act was bloody awful. But I finished strong.
And what's more, the applause was very big. I
didn't realize that this was because the audience
felt sorry for me. I figured that out for myself
later on. At any rate, it was my first time before a
live audience, and I felt good.'*

STAN ON HIS FIRST PERFORMANCE, 1906

FACING PAGE: *Stan Laurel was born with a love of the theatre in his veins.*

TRADITIONALLY, English comedians are either Cockneys or Lancastrians. Of course there are exceptions, but it is strange how many comics come from London or Lancashire. Stan Laurel was born Arthur Stanley Jefferson in 1890 in the north Lancashire town of Ulverston, which lies in the promontory of Furness, north of Morecambe Bay, an area of mines, furnaces and quarries. He spent his early years there in the house of his mother's parents. In his highly peripatetic existence, this, his first home, was almost his only one of any duration until late in life.

Always called Stan or Stanley, he was born into a theatrical family. His father, Arthur Jefferson (usually known as A.J.), was an impresario, actor and writer, who knew and at one time or another practised every imaginable theatrical craft, from wig-maker to publicity agent. His mother, Madge, was also an actress, described by more than one writer as the 'Theda Bara of northern England'.

Stan's brother, Gordon, followed his father into theatre management, and it was hoped that Stan might do the same. But he, from an early age, was set on being a performer. When he briefly attended a boarding school in Bishop Auckland, he kept some members of the staff amused with after-hours clowning, including mimicry of their colleagues.

According to legend, Stan's first professional appearance came about without his father's help. In 1905 A.J. became manager of a famous theatre in Glasgow, the Metropole. His son Stan, having finally given up on school, where he never excelled, worked in the box office. One afternoon when things were quiet, A.J. strolled down to a neighbouring theatre for a chat with its proprietor, another famous impresario, named Pickard. When he got there, Pickard said to him, 'You're just in time. Stan's on in a minute.' A.J. could not think what he meant, but he was soon

'I don't think playing to Bates and the other masters helped my education any, as I was given a lot of privileges and a lot of my backwardness in class was overlooked, which many times since I've regretted, [but] those were happy days at Bishop Auckland.' STAN'S SCHOOLDAYS

'We [the Jefferson family] were seldom together. I was almost always either in boarding school or living with my grandparents in Ulverston, but still, strange as it may seem, we were always a close family.' STAN'S FAMILY LIFE

RIGHT: *Even as a boy, Stan always played the clown, and relished having an audience.*

'I guess I inherited his red hair, which was always kept in a crew cut. He was a very energetic man, a stylish dresser, and was always referred to as "The Guv'nor". He was a great showman, had a unique flair for advertising his theatres and shows … I can remember once he had a lion cage hauled around the streets with a real lion in it mauling a body. The body wasn't real, of course — just a fully dressed dummy with a big piece of meat inside. When crowds gathered around the waggon, canvas signs would drop down reading, "Tonight! At the Theatre Royal!"'

STAN ON HIS FATHER, THE IMPRESARIO

enlightened. He recognized the 'boy comedian' (there was a fashion for them at that time: Charlie Chaplin was currently touring with the 'Lancashire Lads') who now appeared on the stage. And he also recognized the boy comedian's clothes, including the hacked-off trousers belonging to one of

'I dabbled around [in his father's theatres], some nights in the box office, some nights checking programmes and selling chocolates — general utility, message boy, etc. I went to see music-hall shows. I had quite a lisp at the time, my voice was broken and I wasn't fitting for anything but a comic, so I decided that was my forte. Anyway, my Dad found out that was my desire and got me a job with Levy and Cardwell [a pantomime troupe].' BACKSTAGE JOBS

his own best suits. Like his son, A.J. was at heart a genial fellow. When Stan got home, A.J. said nothing about the ruined suit. He congratulated Stan on his act and offered him a whisky and soda.

In 1907 A.J. introduced Stan to a company currently touring with a pantomime, *Sleeping Beauty,* and Stan Jefferson was launched on his career as a comedian. It was a rough life, working as a comic in provincial Edwardian music halls. The artists were constantly on the move, living in cheap

LEFT: *Stan was a great admirer of Charlie Chaplin, and toured with him in Fred Karno's troupe.*

RIGHT: *Stan Laurel (right) sharing a joke with Fred Karno (middle) and Hal Roach (left).*

lodgings and, since pay was low and job security nonexistent, they often went hungry. Stan was once reduced to stealing a loaf of bread. But those who, like Stan, were talented enough to survive in this trade were devoted to it. They could not know that the music hall would soon enter a terminal decline, nor could they guess that its traditions would be carried on, by Charlie Chaplin and Stan in particular, into the new medium which replaced it.

The 'king' of variety in England in the years before the First World War was Fred Karno, who 'talent-spotted' Stan in 1910. Stan was, for a time, Charlie Chaplin's understudy.

Both Stan and Charlie toured North America with Karno's troupe in 1910. For a time they shared lodgings in West 43rd Street, New York, but they were never close. Stan is not mentioned in Charlie's autobiography. Professional jealousy – Charlie's ambition and intolerance of rivals were legendary – may have been the reason. But there was no bad blood. Although Stan did not hit the big time until many years after Charlie, he never had a bad word to say about him, publicly at least. 'Charlie was, is, and will be always the greatest comedian in the world', he once said.

'*When you're travelling, we had to pay our own sleepers, hotels, food and what have you, and even though everything was very cheap at that time, still twenty dollars wasn't enough to travel on and take care of yourself, so it ended up with three or four of us sharing a room.*'

ON TOURING AMERICA WITH THE KARNO TROUPE

When Charlie was signed up by Mack Sennett, the famous producer of the frenetic Keystone comedies, in the middle of a second tour in 1912, Karno let him go (he had originally signed him up at £3.50 a week; Sennett was offering $125). Stan decided to try his luck as a freelance in America. With a husband and wife team from the Karno company, he put together a sketch called *The Nutty Burglars,* which was good enough to attract an excellent agent, Gordon Bostock. With his brother Claude, Bostock was to look after Stan's affairs for many years. Sometimes the money was good, though never so good that Stan didn't spend it all in rapid time, a lot of it on bottles. In Philadelphia in 1916 he took up with Mae Dahlberg. He left his current partners somewhat in the lurch, though such was his innocent charm they did not hold it against him, even when he pinched the act as well.

Mae was a big, brassy Australian. Although Stan was soon referring to her as 'the hag' and the noises of their quarrelling shook the flimsy walls of many a dressing room, they remained inextricably entangled for many years. It was at this time that Stan adopted the name Laurel. The main reason for the change was that 'Stan Jefferson' contains thirteen letters. Like most show people, Stan was superstitious.

Adolph Ramish, who owned a theatre in Los Angeles where Stan and Mae were performing, was the first to see movie potential in Stan Laurel. Remarking that in his opinion Stan was funnier than Chaplin, Ramish put up the money for a one-reeler starring Stan and Mae. It was called *Nuts in May,* Stan's first film, released in 1917. Chaplin, then about to set up his own studio, saw the film and liked it. He and Stan had dinner together and talked of professional cooperation. At that time Stan was not as we think of him now; he was a quite different kind of comedian, much more in Chaplin's mode, faster and physically more active than the Stan we know best. He was, in fact, very like Chaplin in technique, and one of his vaudeville acts had been a Chaplin impersonation. When Chaplin failed to follow up their meeting, Stan signed a year's contact with Universal. He made several shorts playing a character called Hickory Hiram, a sort of village idiot. As a result of studio reorganization, his contract was cancelled before the year was up.

BABE

'I like to watch people. Once in a while someone will ask me where Stan and I dreamed up the characters we play in the movies. They seem to think that these two fellows aren't like anybody else. I know they're DUMBER than anyone else, but there are plenty of Laurels and Hardys in the world. Whenever I travel, I still am in the habit of sitting in the lobby and watching the people walk by — and I tell you I see many Laurels and Hardys.'

Unlike Stan Laurel, Oliver Hardy had no background in show business of any kind. Oliver Norvell Hardy was born in Harlem, Georgia, in 1892, the youngest of six children, a handsome baby (it's easy to imagine) who was adored by his older sisters. Oliver Hardy senior was a lawyer, who died when Oliver, or rather Norvell as he was known as a child, was ten years old. There is some disagreement as to whether he was named Oliver at birth or adopted his father's name later; Norvell was his mother's maiden name. Years later, in the films, he would use his full name to introduce his character because it sounded impressive, saying something like, 'I am Oliver Norvell Hardy, and this is my friend Mr Stanley Laurel.'

The Hardy family was comfortably off, though less so after his father's death, and Ollie's famous courtliness of manner, a vital ingredient of his comic persona, came natu-

RIGHT: *Always the Southern gentleman, Oliver Hardy was adored by his older sisters — and by many other women in later life.*

> '*It appears to me as if I never really made up my mind to do anything very definite. I did want to be a lawyer for a while and studied for a bit at the University of Georgia, but I gave that up.*'
>
> BABE'S YOUTHFUL AMBITIONS

'I saw some of the comedies that were being made [around 1910-13] and I thought to myself that I could be as good — or maybe as BAD — as some of those boys. So I gave up the movie theatre and went to Jacksonville, Florida. I started to work for Lubin Motion Pictures. I made five dollars a day — with three days work a week guaranteed.'

MR HARDY JOINS THE FILM BUSINESS

rally to him as a Southern gentleman. The family was also fond of music and young Oliver had a beautiful treble voice, and later, an equally fine tenor. He must have caught the performing bug young, because when he was only eight years old he spent a short period touring with an outfit known as Coburn's Minstrels. Later he studied at the Conservatory of Music in Atlanta. He also attended a military school and, briefly, the University of Georgia, but soon gave up his plan to follow his father into the law.

After his father's death, Oliver's mother ran a hotel in Madison, Georgia, where he spent many hours watching the comings and goings of the guests from a chair in the lobby. Though unaware of it at the time, he must have built up useful knowledge of the idiosyncrasies of human behaviour.

In 1910 he acquired a movie theatre in nearby Midgeville, one of the first in the area. Watching the jerky, flickering comedies, he concluded that he was at the wrong end of the business. He sold his movie theatre and went to Jacksonville, Florida, where there were one or two film studios. He sang in a nightclub in the town at night and worked in films in the day. He also acquired a wife, a singer named Madelyn Saloshin, who was far more successful than he. This may have been the reason why, although they didn't divorce till much later, the marriage lasted only three or four years.

In films at this time Babe was usually cast as a 'heavy' — a villain (though usually a comic villain) — a term that in this case can be taken literally as well as metaphorically. He was always a big man — around 127 kg (280 pounds), in his prime and 188 cm (six feet two inches) tall. Although he was undeniably fat, and his love of food helped him stay like that, he was not flabby. Apart from the double chins, he was solid. He was fond of games, played football when young and

adored playing golf when he was older. As anyone who has watched the films must have noticed, he was surprisingly agile and light on his feet. He was, in fact, a very good dancer.

LEFT: *Comic roles seemed more abundant than straight parts for a man of Hardy's proportions.*

'I never really tried to cut down and, of course, after Stan and I got known as fat and skinny, it just wasn't smart to cut down on my weight. But for many years there when we did our pictures, I wasn't really fat. I've always been big. I'm big-boned. Everyone in my family was big.'

BABE ON BEING A BIG MAN

Though he could scarcely be called successful, Babe got plenty of work — small character roles mostly in comedy shorts. In the early 1920s he must have been employed by almost every active studio and, although his true talent was never spotted until Hal Roach and Leo McCarey put him together with Stan Laurel, he became a very efficient and reliable actor. His range of

RIGHT: *Laurel and Hardy worked together in a number of films before becoming a recognized team.*

parts may have been limited by his remarkable size, but there were more than enough to keep him eating – and Babe liked to eat. Although there is no evidence, it seems possible that Babe's original decision to go into films was partly made because there were a lot of parts in the current slapstick comedies for a man of his dimensions.

He always regarded himself as an actor rather than a comedian, and although he seldom did anything funny – as distinct from simply *being* funny – in the Laurel and Hardy films, his was much the more striking presence. Stan may have been the creative one, the ideas man always thinking up a new gag, but Ollie was the 'bigger' character in every way.

Babe went to California in 1918. He was hired to play yet another comic heavy, delivering such lines as 'Put 'em up, insect, before I comb your hair with lead', and get into situations such as being stuck in a hole in a fence in a position allowing the hero to kick him vigorously in the butt. The hero was played by a comedian who had also been around for some time. He had attracted Anderson with his vulnerable-simpleton appeal, which made audiences sympathize with him as well as laugh at him. His name was Stan Laurel.

'*Well, here's another fine mess you've got me into!*'
OLLIE'S PUNCHLINE

MR LAUREL AND MR HARDY

'Please don't say my friend Babe and I have ever had a word. Babe is one of my best friends and the only arguments we have had have been an occasional difference of opinion on stories. There isn't an actor in the world who doesn't want to discuss a story idea and give his own personal viewpoint.' STAN TO GOSSIP COLUMNIST LOUELLA PARSONS (1935)

FACING PAGE: *PUTTING PANTS ON PHILIP was the first true 'Laurel and Hardy' film.*

'Keeping us under separate contract meant that he [Roach] could control us completely, bargain with each of us individually. Whereas if we were a team contractually, if we were a legal entity, he would find it much more difficult to manoeuvre a deal to his special advantage. Now, I don't mean Hal was ever dishonest with us, or tried to gyp us. We were always well paid. But we could have made more money and had greater freedom if we had been legally a team long before we were [in 1940].' STAN'S RELATIONS WITH HAL ROACH

WHEN PEOPLE TALK about the early makers of film comedies, the first name mentioned is usually Mack Sennett, originator of the Keystone Kops. In some ways Hal Roach was just as important. Sennett tended to have most of the top stars, among them, for a while, Chaplin. Roach's operation was less glamorous, though in fact, he had started off with Harold Lloyd as his partner. Lloyd made more money than either Chaplin or Keaton in the 1920s, but he left Roach as soon as he became really successful.

Hal Roach was born in the same week as Babe Hardy, and physically he was not unlike a trimmed-down version of the actor. He came from a poor background, and had worked as a truck driver before he drifted into the nascent film business in 1914. When he inherited a modest legacy, he teamed up with Harold Lloyd to produce movies. He had a good eye for talent, even though it took a long time for him to spot the chemistry of Laurel and Hardy, and he was quick to think of comic situations, though he preferred to let others turn idea into act. 'That's the idea, boys,' he would say. 'Work it out, know what I mean?' His energy and his ebullient self-confidence are plainly evident even in photographs. He also had deceptive intelligence and – unusually for a studio boss – an easy-going nature.

Both Stan and Babe worked for Roach many years before he signed them to long-term contracts. Until 1940 they never had a joint contract. As they were signed up at different times, their contracts never came up for renewal on the same date. As a result they couldn't mount a united front in their negotiations, a fact that Stan in particular came to resent.

One necessity for success as a star of comic films was to establish a known character. Roach was undoubtedly aware of Stan's talents, but perhaps he wasn't sure how to use him. He did have other money-spinners in the early twenties, including the kids of 'Our Gang' and a comic called Charley Chase, to whom Stan and Babe gave occasional support. It may be that the presence of Mae Dahlberg bothered Roach. His views on morals were on the puritanical side, but even if he had no objection to Stan and Mae living in sin, he had no wish to employ Mae, only Stan. Unfortunately, it was very difficult to get one without the other.

Lots of people remarked, then or later, that Mae was a drag on Stan's career. She was a more powerful character than he, and

'I fell in with Joe Rock, a comedian in his own right, who got the idea of making and producing comedies for himself … Gosh, those were fun to make! Joe went to Universal for studio space and in his rental agreement he stipulated that he could use any of the old Universal sets still in shape. Some of those sets were massive – like the huge set for THE HUNCHBACK OF NOTRE DAME, *the picture that starred Lon Chaney at his height. We took that gorgeous set and used it for a two-reel take-off on* DR JEKYLL AND MR HYDE. *We called it* DR PYCKLE AND MR PRYDE …'*

STAN ON HIS DAYS WITH JOE ROCK

although he could shout back, in the end he could never stand up to her. There was another problem: Stan always had a weakness for the bottle, and when he was unhappy, he drank more. Roach would have been aware of that.

However, there were other producers who appreciated Stan's talents. 'Broncho Billy' Anderson was one. Another was Joe Rock, who had also been a performer —

part of an acrobatic comedy team called Rock and Montgomery – before he became a producer. Rock not only gave Stan work, he got Mae out of his hair. Joe told Stan he wanted to hire him for a series of films, but he did not want to hire the other half of his vaudeville act, that is, Mae. Stan at first agreed, but soon collapsed under pressure from Mae. Joe Rock boldly tackled her himself. He told her she was holding Stan back

BELOW: *A scene from* LEAVE *'EM LAUGHING (1928).*

and, with the aid of a handsome bribe, he persuaded her to go home to Australia, where she had been born and where she still had a husband. Strangely, Mae went without too much protest. All the same, Joe wisely arranged to have the money held by the purser until the ship was a day's sail clear of New York.

Early in 1926 Roach lured him away from Rock, but as a writer and director rather than an actor. Rock had apparently agreed to this, but Stan also, inevitably, became involved on the performing side, and a legal wrangle ensued. The upshot was, however, that Stan signed with Roach. (Joe Rock went bust in the Great Crash three years later, moved to England and set himself up again there.)

There is little doubt that Laurel and Hardy would never have happened if they had not been employed by Hal Roach. The Roach studio was comparatively small. In a business sense it was, from 1927, part of the empire of MGM, which distributed all the Roach films. Otherwise, it was totally self-contained. In the early years especially, it gave an impression, corny though it sounds, of one big happy family. Roach had moved his parents in, and they lived in the lower part of a building where script conferences

took place; access to the office was sometimes obscured by lines of washing.

There was not much evidence of the 'star system' here either. After Laurel and Hardy became big stars, it is said that everyone and everything was organized to keep them, especially Stan, happy, but a lot of the apparent fuss seems to have been humorous. Stan quite enjoyed being treated as a big shot, but he took it more or less in fun. He was the opposite of a snob; if anything, he could be called an inverted snob. It is interesting to compare him with Charlie Chaplin

> '... *Funny thing about that cry, though: it's the only mannerism I ever used in the films that I didn't like. ... When we would be improvising something on the set and we came to a pause where we couldn't think of anything to do ... Roach always insisted that I use the cry. It always got a laugh, and it sure became a part of my standard equipment, but somehow I never had any affection for it.'* STAN'S 'CRY'

in this respect. Charlie became quite fond of mixing with the rich and famous, but his political views remained notoriously left-wing. Stan, equally devoted in his way to 'the people', was a great admirer of Franklin D. Roosevelt and of John F. Kennedy, but in his later years he was firmly conservative. Babe too; though it must be said that neither of them was that much interested in politics.

One of Stan's first jobs after joining the company in 1926 was to direct a two-reeler called *Get 'Em Young,* in Roach's successful 'Comedy All Stars' series, in which films were churned out at the rate of one a month. Babe had a part in this as a butler. Just as filming was about to begin, Babe, who like all true gourmets was a keen and talented cook, slipped while basting a roast in his kitchen at home and scalded himself badly. It sounds like the sort of thing that might happen in a Laurel and Hardy film, but in real life such mishaps have more serious consequences, and Babe had to call off. Roach asked Stan to step in and do the part himself. For some reason Stan was very reluctant, but, after much persuasion and a rise in pay, he agreed.

When Babe recovered, Roach decided to cast him and Stan together. In their first film, which was based on an old sketch by Stan's father, *Home from the Honeymoon,* Babe was again cast as a butler, Stan as a highly incompetent maid. But this was not yet Laurel and Hardy either. Some of the ingredients were there. They were both, for instance, exceedingly stupid. Stan evolved one of his famous mannerisms, the babyish 'cry', in which his eyes screw up, his mouth gets even wider, and his chin even longer. Half a dozen more shorts followed in quick time. The Roach studio may have been more laid back than most, but it operated at an equally rapid rate.

Roach and Leo McCarey, who was an important influence on their development, both recognized the potential in the team, but they had no established characters. In more than one of these films Babe wore a beard. Everything – well, almost everything – clicked into place when Roach asked McCarey to supervise future Laurel and Hardy productions. Their first film (first to be made, but second to be released) under this new arrangement was also the first true 'Laurel and Hardy' film. It was called, none too inspiringly, *Putting Pants on Philip*. 'Philip', that is, Stan (they had not yet adopted their own names), is a young Scot who arrives in America in a kilt to the dismay of his uncle, Ollie, who is obviously anxious to see him in trousers.

It is hard to say exactly what the decisive changes were, or to what extent they were due to McCarey, to Stan, or to others. They had not yet adopted their characteristic costume of 'derby' (bowler) hats and winged collars, though they did soon afterwards. Some other bits of business, soon to become familiar, were already in place, such as Ollie's conspiracy with the audience by means of a direct gaze into the camera. He exploited this dangerous device brilliantly, his mood and his expression varying, but

'So many good things for me came out of the same film [WHY GIRLS LOVE SAILORS] … Just after I did the tie-twiddle, I had to become very exasperated. So I just stared right into the camera and registered disgust. The camera kept on going, and in that way my slow burn was born.' [Babe's memory wasn't quite accurate: he had used his 'camera look' before.]

'As far as make-up goes, I emphasized my lack of brains by making my face as blank as possible. I used very light make-up and made my eyes smaller by lining the inner lids. Babe, in keeping with his wish to obtain an even BIGGER kind of dignity, combed his hair down in a spit-curls bangs effect. This was in perfect harmony with his elegant nature and those fancy-dan gestures of his.'

'There is just so much comedy we can do along a certain line and then it gets to be unfunny. You've got to settle for a simple basic story in our case and then work out all the comedy that's there — and then let it alone.'

most often conveying exquisite exasperation. McCarey was also to claim responsibility for a much more significant innovation: a change in pace.

Early comedies had thrived on frenetic, nonstop action. In fact, the Keystone comedies seem, to our eyes, to consist of little else. In Laurel and Hardy, everything is deliberately slowed down. When Ollie, carrying an enormous cream cake, slips on a banana skin and ends up flat on the floor with his face buried in the cake, he simply lies there prostrate for several long seconds – while the audience's laughter builds. The most manic destruction proceeds in a sort of ritualistic calm

One of the difficulties in performing comedy on film rather than on stage is that, in the absence of an audience, it is difficult to know how to gauge the length of the laughter after each gag. Stan and his colleagues used to show a few previews to see how the laughter went and then re-edited accordingly. Hardy's long gaze of exasperation or resignation straight at the camera following the perpetration of some frightful act by Stan was extremely useful. The audience would laugh at Stan's act, and also at Ollie's reaction. Ollie's 'camera look' could be maintained indefinitely, and it could therefore be cut to the time suggested by the laughter of the preview audience.

'The Ollie Hardy character was partly based on "Helpful Henry"... a cartoon character in Georgia newspapers when I was a boy. He was always trying to be helpful but he was always making a mess of things. He was very big and fussy and important, but underneath it all he was a very nice guy. That's very much like the character I play.'

SHORT AND SILENT

'Our prime worry was whether or not the picture was going to be good. The studio didn't bother us much if at all about a schedule because we didn't have a lot of people in our casts as a rule. There weren't any unions, and people just worked until we got the effects we wanted.'

'*After the picture was assembled, we previewed it and if no re-takes were needed, we started to prepare the next story ... If Roach was anxious for us to get started, we'd go into production almost right away after finishing a picture, and complete the script as we went along. We would start out with an idea, go along working on it as we were shooting, and then we would frequently deviate from the original idea. We worked hard, but there was no real pressure. It was fun, particularly in the silent days.*'

IN 1927 LAUREL AND HARDY made thirteen films, in 1928 they made eleven. These films were all silent, and they were all two-reelers (one reel of cinematic film is about 300 metres, or 1000 feet, long; running time is variable, but roughly ten minutes). Short films of this type went out as supporting features, but Laurel and Hardy were soon so popular that their two-reelers received equal billing with the main feature. By the 1930s they were sometimes billed above the main feature.

BELOW: *THE HOOSEGOW was one of Laurel and Hardy's outstanding shorts, directed by James Parrott — possibly the best of their directors.*

Turning out films at such a rate suggests that Roach worked to a very strict schedule but, according to Stan, in the early days this was not the case. Casts and crews were small: teamwork ensured that films were completed on time. The rate of production did mean that, compared with the modern industry, techniques were fairly primitive. The camera was usually stationary. Takes were often very long by modern standards. This made great demands on the actors, especially when engaged in slapstick routines, where physical agility is demanded. Retakes were few. Films were made in the studio or outside (it seems pretentious to describe scenes in the street outside or in the local park as 'on location'), or both.

A common scenario was three scenes; for example, in *The Hoosegow* (1929): (1) Stan and Ollie arriving at prison, (2) at work in the prison, (3) the obligatory terminal scene of comic violence, in this case a tremendous fight with cooked rice. Laurel and Hardy gags often obey a similar, triad form. The joke is repeated three times with variations and, usually, the third and final version ends in destruction or disaster. In *The Finishing Touch,* Ollie is house-building. He wishes to transport a door frame across a gap to the first floor, and places a plank across the gap. As he is about to step on to the plank, it is removed by the empty-headed Stan. Ollie falls. Stan, as always anxious to make amends, helpfully reconstructs the bridge with double planks, but the bottom plank is very thin and the top one is divided in two. Ollie falls. A third attempt is made to reconstruct the bridge, and this time Ollie carefully tests it first. He strides confidently across, with a 'Ha! Fooled you!' look at the camera. As he reaches the other side, the whole building collapses. Ollie falls.

BELOW: *1930 was a relatively unproductive period for Stan and Babe; ANOTHER FINE MESS was one of only seven films made that year.*

The essential Stan and Ollie relationship was established as early as *Putting Pants on Philip*. The Hardy character here is a very proper, small-town gent, who is dragged into highly embarrassing situations by his

---

'We actually had to stop shooting one day because we were laughing so much. I broke up Babe, and he broke me up. We finally had to call it a day when it got too much for us.'

---

brainless and accident-prone nephew, visiting him from Scotland. There is a lot of play with kilts and what is or is not worn beneath them. This seems less funny now, but audiences then had not, like us, seen it all many times before. One little scene, in retrospect, is very typical Laurel and Hardy fun. The nephew, Stan, who in spite of general timidity is an obsessive girl-chaser, lays down his kilt over a puddle in front of a pretty girl, in the manner of Sir Walter Raleigh. She ignores him and passes on without stepping on the kilt. 'Uncle Piedmont' (Hardy) is amused, and plans to

show his nephew how a smoother performer approaches a pretty girl. He does this with full Southern charm and gallantry, only to be thoroughly disconcerted when the girl flicks him vulgarly on the nose and flounces off. He turns on his suppressed-exasperation expression.

This is not the end of it. Laurel and Hardy jokes always build, as one disaster follows another. Recrossing the road, Hardy decides that he will make use of the kilt. He steps on it and immediately sinks into mud right up to his neck.

In their early films they adopt many different sorts of role, such as convicts, sailors and waiters, but their characters are established as 'Stan' and 'Ollie'. As in all good comedy, characterization is vital and, like all good comedians, Laurel and Hardy do not grow less funny (rather the reverse) when you have a fairly exact notion of what they are going to do, how they are going to behave or what happens next.

A typical example is *The Battle of the Century*. One of their funniest films, it also follows the three-act formula. In this film Stan is a boxer (this was the year of the notorious Dempsey–Tunney fight, billed as the 'battle of the century', which was won by Tunney after he had survived a knock-

'It brought the pie throwing to apotheosis. There was nothing but pie-throwing in it, nothing but pies, thousands and thousands of pies ...'

HENRY MILLER

down thanks to an extra-long count). Ollie is his manager. The battle, however, has nothing to do with the boxing.

As may be imagined, Stan is a hopeless boxer. The first scene shows him being knocked cold by the first blow he receives, provoking a characteristic look of infinite resignation from his manager. Someone suggests that, since Stan is so likely to get injured, Ollie should take out insurance on him. He does so. There follow Hardy's efforts to involve Laurel in an accident — efforts that invariably culminate with Hardy, not Laurel, on the receiving end.

It's the finale that provides the real battle. This is a custard-pie fight. Now this was very old hat even in 1927. According to Stan's recollections thirty years later, when one of his 'ideas men' originally suggested they might 'throw a few pies', he was derisively shouted down. According to another account, it was the chance arrival of a mobile pie-seller on the lot at lunch-time that sparked off the idea.

Anyhow, after further consideration, Stan decided to go ahead with it. But, as he said, if they were going to indulge in a pie fight, they had better make it the biggest and best one ever!

So it was. According to John McCabe, the studio bought up the total day's output from the Los Angeles Pie Company — 4,000 pies in total — and these were genuine fruit pies, made of cherries, bananas and blueberries, not the usual mock pies made largely of foam. This may sound a bit like a well-polished legend, but why should we be sceptics?

'Look, if we make a pie picture [BATTLE OF THE CENTURY], let's make a pie picture to end all pie pictures. Let's give them so many pies that there will never be room for any more pie pictures in the whole history of the movies.'

STAN CONSIDERS A PIE FIGHT

FACING PAGE: *Two Tars features some fine scenes of destruction: the boys play two sailors who create havoc in a traffic jam.*

Motor cars were very useful props in silent comedy, and Laurel and Hardy used them often. A huge fleet of Model T Fords was kept on the Roach lot, but not many of them were in running order. Some were already heaps of scrap, for use in the last scene, where destruction is total. Others were cunningly held together with wire, so they would collapse in pieces at a given moment. One was cut in half so neatly that it appeared whole until the two halves suddenly separated.

Exhilarating scenes of destruction perhaps appeal more to men than women. Since the rise of modern feminism, that must surely be true of Laurel and Hardy's comedy in general. It belonged to a comic tradition in which women, unless young and pretty enough to be flirted with, are generally hostile creatures – bossy wives, hideous mothers-in-law or grotesque fat ladies destined for victimization. It was a tradition Laurel and Hardy did little to moderate, and though Ollie was far too much of a gentleman to actually strike a woman, Stan was prepared, if provoked, to give her a pie in the face or even a kick up the bottom.

There is at least one exception to Ollie's forbearance: a scene in which Stan strikes Ollie's wife, whereupon Ollie retaliates by striking, not Stan, but Stan's wife! This is a characteristic piece of Laurel and Hardy's lunatic logic – also, feminist critics might point out, a further indication that in Laurel and Hardy's world, women are not quite human. They are sometimes allowed just a trace of sympathy, but no more than can be extended to the put-upon cops, landlords, prison governors and other victims of Stan and Ollie's activities.

Because Hal Roach's company was like a repertory theatre company, and its mem-

RIGHT: *Helpmates (1932) rates among Laurel and Hardy's finest films.*

LEFT: *Women often had thankless roles in Laurel and Hardy films, usually cast as nagging wives or hostile mothers-in-law, as in this scene from* THEIR FIRST MISTAKE *(1932).*

bers stuck to the studio to an extent that was perhaps unique in Hollywood, the same players appear in film after film.

A shopkeeper in *Liberty,* made towards the end of 1928, is played by James Finlayson, the most famous of all Stan and Ollie's opponents. The bald-headed, mobile-eyebrowed master of the 'double-take and fade away' (involving contortions difficult to describe but unmistakable when seen) was universally known as 'Fin'. He had come over from Scotland in a variety troupe, like Stan, and about the same time (1911). He was one of the original Keystone Kops, and at one time Roach had high hopes of him. He never quite made it as a star in his own right, but he proved a great asset to Laurel and Hardy.

In the often thankless roles of women, there were, in the early films, Dorothy Coburn and, later, the long-suffering Mae Busch, often condemned to play Mrs Hardy. Anita Garvin as Stan's wife, for instance in *Blotto* (1930), was equally formidable.

These were the faces audiences saw, but, of course, the people behind the scenes were equally important. Leo McCarey probably deserves more credit than anyone except Stan himself for the evolution of the Laurel and Hardy characters. James Parrott, brother of the comedian Charley Chase, was possibly the best of their directors. At any rate, he was responsible for such outstanding shorts as *Two Tars, The Perfect Day* (the most unsuccessful picnic in movie history), *The Hoosegow, Helpmates,* and the Oscar-winning *The Music Box.*

Numerous writers were involved. Some of them were hangers-on of Stan's whom Hal Roach seems to have hired mainly to keep Stan happy. Indeed, Roach himself, though considered by some to have hindered Stan's career at a later stage, deserves perhaps more credit than anyone. Not least of his achievements was that, for most of the time, he kept everybody content.

A few notable stars also took part in Laurel and Hardy films (behind the screen too – an early cameraman was the future director George Stevens). *Liberty* is notable for, besides other reasons, what seems to have been the first appearance in movies of Jean Harlow, most fascinating of all Hollywood's glamorous blondes. Harlow is also in *Double Whoopee* (1929), in which she suffers the indignity of having her dress torn off after a careless hotel porter (guess who!) has caught the hem in the door of a taxi.

RIGHT: *Stan and Ollie also made foreign-language versions of their films, reading the dialogue from idiot boards.*

FACING PAGE: *An heir to Oliver Hardy's comic crown? A still from* TIT FOR TAT *(1935).*

LEARNING TO TALK

'There's nothing really funny about a guy falling downstairs. There's pain connected with it and that's never funny. I realized, of course, that you can take away the sting by not having the man really hurt, but there's nothing real about that. In that scene we REMOVED the pain by having the camera stay looking at the top of the staircase. The sound effect of the fall lets the audience visualize its own scene, and that just made it funnier to them.'

FACING PAGE: *A famous scene from* LIBERTY, *in which Laurel and Hardy are stranded on top of a partially constructed skyscraper.*

THE COMING OF SOUND was probably the biggest trauma in Hollywood's history, bigger even than television. As everyone knows, several top stars proved incapable of making the switch. It wasn't simply that they had inadequate speaking voices; the 'talkies' demanded a quite different style of acting. In silent films the actors are essentially mimes, and to our eyes their acting style seems absurdly exaggerated. The dialogue has to be flashed up on the screen as 'titles', interrupting the action. A wise director kept the titles to a minimum.

Silent comedy would seem, superficially, to be especially vulnerable to the coming of sound. There is much evidence to suggest the truth of this. Charlie Chaplin could not bring himself to speak on film for over a decade, though when at last he did, it worked quite smoothly. Laurel and Hardy, people might have thought, were also threatened. They were no less dependent on mime than Chaplin, and their voices – Stan's slight Lancashire accent, Babe's easy Southern inflections – were slightly unexpected. They were, in fact, the last of Roach's teams to go over to sound. But although they were certainly wary, they do not seem to have been very worried. Nor need they have been.

Laurel and Hardy did not make the mistake of changing their style. They remained the same pair of endearing imbeciles they had always been, with Ollie always rather formal, even in the most undignified circumstances.

In their silent films, titles were relatively few and they were often witty. In one of their 'convict' pictures, for example, the opening shot shows them immured in a police cell. The title comes up: 'Neither Mr Laurel nor Mr Hardy had any thoughts of doing wrong ...' followed by 'As a matter of fact, they had no thoughts of any kind.' Stan and his colleagues exploited sound in a similar way. They used it to augment the comedy without holding up the action.

Some of the ways in which sound could be used to improve a gag seem tediously obvious now but, of course, they were far from obvious when sound was new. In one of their first sound shorts, Hardy hits Laurel over the head with some kind of blunt instrument. A tremendous clang is emitted, like hitting a dustbin with a hammer. They also used sound effectively to prolong a 'series gag' – where the same thing keeps happening in slightly different, cumulatively funnier ways. One example occurs in the original version of *Hog Wild* (1930). Ollie is

'Each time a different gag variation appeared, until the comedy passed into the realm of cutting, and the final fall was but a flight of birds and the sound of a mighty splash. Even Eisenstein would have been proud to do it.'
DIRECTOR-CRITIC BASIL WRIGHT ON OLLIE'S *HOG WILD* ANTICS

trying to put up a radio aerial on the roof of his house. He continually falls off the roof into a goldfish pond. The final fall is heard but not seen — and gets the biggest laugh.

Hal Roach first suggested using sound on *Liberty,* which was made towards the end of 1928 and released in early 1929. It had sound effects but no dialogue. It did, therefore, have titles, and, as usual, they were good. The film begins with a kind of collage of historical events relating to the American colonists' fight for freedom. Up comes a title on the screen: 'Even today, the fight for liberty continues.' Shot of Stan and Ollie, dressed as convicts, trying to make a break from prison.

The first Laurel and Hardy talkie was wittily titled *Unaccustomed As We Are* (1929). It was standard fare, with Ollie and Stan cooking the dinner after Ollie's infuriated wife (Mae Busch) has walked out on them. Naturally, they succeed in blowing up the kitchen. Also involved are Thelma Todd, another talented blonde comedienne, and Edgar Kennedy, doing his suspicious-policeman act. No one complained about the voices, nor did anyone complain that dialogue made the gags slightly fewer or slightly slower.

After *Unaccustomed As We Are,* Laurel and Hardy continued to make two-reelers, but they made only one more silent. However, some of the films of that period had sound effects only — no dialogue — while others were apparently made in both sound and silent versions. As their popularity spread, Laurel and Hardy also made foreign-language versions, in French, German, Spanish and Italian. They read the dialogue from idiot boards. Since Stan and Babe were no linguists, the words were written on the boards phonetically. This practice was discontinued soon after they began making feature-length films.

The coming of sound meant that the team needed new helpers, new talent.

Marvin Hatley, a piano-player and former band-leader with a Sullivanesque talent for pastiche, was a big asset. One day he was fooling around at the piano with a phrase like the call of a cuckoo. Stan came in and said 'I like that.' The eventual result was the 'Cuckoo' song that became a Laurel and Hardy signature tune.

And, of course, now Stan and Ollie could not only speak, they could sing too! In idle moments at the studio, they sometimes put together a barbershop quartet, often with Charley Chase, who, like Babe, had a good singing voice, and Leo McCarey or, later, Marvin Hatley. Stan sang either basso

'I like that thing. I think it's funny. We'll use it in my picture. The top part will be Babe Hardy and the cuckoo part will be me.'

ON FIRST HEARING THE 'CUCKOO' THEME

profondo or falsetto. Considering, for example, the success of 'On the Trail of the Lonesome Pine', they did not do as much singing as they might have done.

In the year 1929 they made thirteen

two-reelers, and also appeared in *The Hollywood Revue of 1929,* a piece of MGM publicity showing off the studio's current stars. It was a vintage year too, including several of their very best shorts. Outstanding among the former was *Big Business,* perhaps their most famous short after *The Music Box.* In *Big Business,* described in the opening title as 'The story of a man who turned the other cheek — and got punched on the nose', Stan and Ollie are Christmas-tree salesmen. The snag is that they are trying to do business in California in August. Another snag is that the proprietor of the second house they call at turns out to be James Finlayson at his most aggressive.

War soon breaks out. Fin destroys their sample Christmas tree with a pair of shears. Ollie responds by attacking his hair, what there is of it, in the same manner. Violence builds. While Fin totally smashes their car, they destroy his house. In the customary Laurel and Hardy manner, the destruction is carried out in an orderly manner, one side standing and watching the other until it is their turn.

In the midst of the war, a policeman (Tiny Sanford) arrives. He is totally bewildered, and certainly the situation doesn't have much sense to it. When he does try to

FACING PAGE: *Stan and Babe make music with Charley Chase.*

ABOVE: *In BIG BUSINESS, James Finlayson (centre) is every salesman's nightmare.*

intervene, Stan and Ollie burst into tears. All are now afflicted with remorse, and everyone, including the large crowd of spectators that has gathered, begins blubbing away heartily. The miscreants hasten to forgive each other. Stan shakes hands with Fin and gives him a cigar. This atmosphere of reconciliation and goodwill is suddenly undermined when Stan and Ollie start gig-

gling. The enraged policeman chases them, while Fin's cigar blows up in his face.

The film was made in a real house, which had at least one unfortunate consequence. According to one story, the actual house that was used was, by some shocking mistake, not the house that Hal Roach had bought for the purpose. It looked like it, but was in the next street. Since the house was completely demolished, it cost the studio a packet in compensation. This, however, is another of those Hollywood legends that we have to make a certain effort to believe.

Among other highlights of 1929 were *Wrong Again* and *Angora Love*. In *Wrong Again* Stan and Ollie do a favour to a millionaire by restoring to him a piece of lost property called 'Blue Boy'. The Blue Boy in question is a painting, but the Blue Boy that Stan and Ollie have got hold of is a horse. The owner is engaged upstairs when the boys arrive, and in answer to their inquiry where they should put Blue Boy he shouts down, 'On the piano!' Fortunately, it's a very well trained horse, so ...

Angora Love stars a goat. It is an illicit goat and must be hidden from the landlord (Edgar Kennedy). When the landlord is heard approaching, Stan and Ollie need a hiding place quickly for the goat. Ollie lifts

FACING PAGE: *Stan and Ollie often shared the stage with animals, as in WRONG AGAIN.*

Left: *The goat jokes in* Angora Love *were recycled, with minor variations, in other films.*

'The picture really had no plot, just that goat — but we sure got a lot of footage out of him. I give a piece of cookie to the goat and he wants more so he follows us around. We try every conceivable way to get rid of him, but no use. We hid — we walked backward — we disguised ourselves. Nothing helped. We finally brought the goat to our room because the word had spread around that the goat had been stolen and we didn't want to be arrested as goatnappers … Later, when sound came, we did a version of the same idea but substituted a chimpanzee for the goat.'

STAN REMEMBERS *ANGORA LOVE*

up the bedspread and points to the space under the bed. Stan lets go of the goat and scrambles under the bed himself. Among other things, this film illustrates how Laurel and Hardy recycle their old material. At their rate of productivity, some creative economy was necessary. The situation in *Angora Love* was to be reworked in *Laughing Gravy* (1931), when the goat's part was played by a dog, and again in *The Chimp* (1932), with a chimpanzee.

The following year, 1930, was less productive. Laurel and Hardy made only seven films, with an appearance in another MGM feature. Domestic troubles were the main cause of this falling off. It is sad that Stan, and to some extent Babe as well, while having a wonderful time making movies, were often unhappy in their personal lives. In 1930 both had incipient marriage problems, and, worse, Stan's wife, Lois, gave birth prematurely to a son, Stan Jr, who lived only nine days. Stan got blind drunk and was off work for nearly three months.

The MGM feature film in which they appeared was called *The Rogue Song*. It was a vehicle for the opera singer Lawrence Tibbett, and was made in a primitive form of Technicolor. Stan and Babe were there to add some comic relief. The script was written for them and they were not allowed to do things their own way. As later experiences were to show, this was always fatal, and by all accounts the comic relief they introduced to *The Rogue Song* was not all that comic and offered little relief. No one can judge now, though, for all copies of the film have, it seems, disappeared.

THE FEATURES

'We should have stayed in the short-film category ... We didn't want to go into feature films in the first place, and even though I've got some favourites among them, I'm sorry we ever did go beyond the two- and three-reelers.'

STAN PREFERS SHORTS

FACING PAGE: *Way Out West was Stan and Ollie's only Western, especially memorable for their singing and dancing.*

A FILM WHICH, in its way, was a no less potent innovator than *The Jazz Singer* was a little item released a few weeks before Christmas in 1928. It was called *Steamboat Willie* and it was the first animated cartoon with sound. It starred a character called Mickey Mouse. The growing popularity of cartoons was an obvious threat to Laurel and Hardy's type of two-reeler comedy: they competed for the same space in the programme.

Cartoons were not the only competition. Perhaps more dangerous was the feeling in the Hollywood of the early to mid-thirties that slapstick comedy had had its day. A new, more sophisticated form of comedy, typified by the films of Frank Capra (who began his career as a writer in the Roach studio), was now seen as the coming thing. Even Hal Roach wanted to move into this field. But, whatever the Hollywood moguls believed, the plain fact was that Stan and Ollie remained very popular.

Hal Roach saw the future of Laurel and Hardy in features. Stan was reluctant to make this move. In a way both were right. Roach was right from the commercial angle, Stan from the artistic one. He thought his type of comedy would be hard-pressed to hold the audience's attention if stretched to an hour or more's running time. He preferred the two-reeler, the film equivalent of a vaudeville sketch.

Laurel and Hardy's first feature film, made in 1931, seemed to bear out Stan's anxieties. It was called *Pardon Us* and started out as a two-reeler, being extended to full length as part of some deal between Roach and MGM. Although it contained one very funny scene at the dentist, on the whole the laughs were spread a lot thinner than in the best of the shorts.

Although *Pardon Us* was not a promising start to Laurel and Hardy's career in feature films, things improved. Their second feature, *Pack Up Your Troubles* (1932), though it has some dreary stretches, was better. It contains the famous scene in which Stan tells a bedtime story to a little girl to help her to sleep. She knows the story and takes over the narration. Stan is lulled to sleep.

Several of their best shorts were released in 1932, among them *County Hospital, Towed in a Hole* and what is probably their best-known film — Stan himself regarded it as their best — *The Music Box*. It was to win an Oscar that year as the Best Live Action Comedy Short Subject. This was Stan and Babe's only Oscar. In old age Stan was to be given one of those general-purpose Oscars that the movie establishment hands out to deserving veterans. Unfortunately, Babe was already dead by then, and Stan was too sick to attend the presentation in person.

The Music Box, a three-reeler, was shot in a few days. It adopted the same plot, or rather the same situation, as the silent two-reeler of 1927, *Hats Off*: two men making a delivery to a house at the top of a long flight of steps. In *The Music Box* the object they have to deliver is a mechanical piano. Although the whole film is very funny, the part that people remember is the first part — the efforts of the two ill-assorted delivery men to get the piano to the house. Everything that can go wrong does, and the whole enterprise proves to have been unnecessary because, when they finally get to the house, they find there is a road leading up to the back. So, with Laurelesque logic, they carry the wretched instrument all the way down again in order to drive it up the road. The image of those stairs, and Stan and Ollie's amazingly incompetent attempts to get the piano up them, seems to sum up the whole art of Laurel and Hardy.

After the award of the Oscar, Stan and Babe took a well-deserved holiday. They had been working hard for six years, though not without a break (Stan had taken a trip to Hawaii), and Stan wanted to visit his old home. Babe decided to go with him. This meant that it was partly a working holiday, as they were to make several public appearances in Europe.

It was on this trip that they discovered just how popular they were, especially in Europe. They also discovered how much they liked each other, for although their professional relationship had always been good, they had not previously had much social contact outside the studio.

LEFT: *Stan and Ollie enjoyed an enormous following in Europe, making French, German, Spanish and Italian versions of their films.*

ABOVE: *With James
Finlayson in THE DEVIL'S
BROTHER (also called FRA
DIAVOLO).*

The intense admiration of their fans was not altogether a happy revelation. Church bells playing the 'Cuckoo' song were one thing, but the public hysteria on several occasions got badly out of hand. In Glasgow thirty people hurt in the crush had to be taken to hospital. All hopes of travelling around as tourists seeing the sights or play-ing golf at St Andrews had to be abandoned. On the whole, it was a relief when, after six hectic weeks, they boarded the ship for New York.

Laurel and Hardy had become stars without noticing it themselves, but there were now more signs of affluence. Stan no longer came to the studio in the morning on a bicycle. He arrived in a large Pierce-Arrow saloon driven by a chauffeur. There was also a yacht – a humble vessel compared with Charlie Chaplin's, but a yacht none the less (Stan was a keen fisherman).

They were still at their best. The year after *The Music Box* came their third feature film *The Devil's Brother,* which in terms of box-office receipts was the most successful film Laurel and Hardy ever made. The film is based, very loosely, on a French opera of 1830 – its nineteenth-century setting suited the boys – and they were present as comic relief. Critics complained that the rest of the movie was not up to much, but the public liked it, and so did Stan and Babe, partly perhaps because they liked dressing up. It is also notable for Stan's 'kneesie-earsie-nosie' routine (slap knees, pull nose with left hand while pulling left ear with right hand, repeat reversing hands). It looks easy, Ollie certainly thinks it is, but when he tries it, he finds he cannot do it. This drives him nuts.

In spite of fame and money, by the mid-thirties there were signs that Stan was becoming restless. Relations with Hal Roach were less than smooth. Personal reasons partly accounted for this. Stan's second marriage was not proving a success and he was drinking heavily. But it seems likely that

'... There's very little to write about me ... Stan can fill you in on all the comedy stuff done in the pictures – and as for my life, it wasn't very exciting and I didn't do very much outside of doing a lot of gags before a camera and play golf the rest of the time.'

Stan was less than entirely happy being so exclusively part of a team. Not that he was unhappy with Babe as a partner – on the contrary. But as a creative artist he felt the need to assert his independence. As for Babe, that blessedly unambitious man, anything Stan said was OK with him.

Hal Roach was inclined to resist Stan's demands, including his demands for more money. Eventually, this was to lead to a break in relations, but it is hard not to think that in many ways Roach was right. He was certainly right that Stan had no sense for business. In view of what happened to Laurel and Hardy after the final break with Roach, he would seem to have been right that they were better off working for him. Still, that break lay far in the future when

ABOVE: *SONS OF THE DESERT*
is one of Laurel and
Hardy's most admired
feature films.

they were making *The Devil's Brother* and,
released the same year, *Sons of the Desert*.

The title of the latter film (also known as
Fraternally Yours) was later to be adopted by
the Laurel and Hardy fan club, since it refers
not to antics in the Sahara, but to a type of
fraternity, an all-male social club. There is
perhaps some dim connection with freema-

sonry — Babe was himself a mason. The plot
concerns the boys' attempt to deceive their
wives into thinking they have gone to
Hawaii for their health and not to the Sons
of the Desert's annual convention in
Chicago. It is much shorter than *The Devil's
Brother* and a proper Laurel and Hardy vehicle, with no boring patches. Some critics,
Charles Barr for example, regard it as the
best of their features: 'deeply funny, with a
great richness of detail, meticulously acted
and plotted, and directed with an understanding of the timing which Laurel and
Hardy's personalities dictate'.

Between 1934 and 1940 Laurel and
Hardy made ten more features for Hal
Roach. The shorts rapidly fell away: four in
1934 (including one gem, *Them Thar Hills*),
three in 1935, none thereafter. The feature
films fell into several different categories.
For example, there were three more in the
same genre as *The Devil's Brother,* based
(none too faithfully) on light opera and not
too far removed from traditional English
pantomime. The best of them is probably
Swiss Miss (1938), which includes another
classic scene comparable with the steps
sequence in *The Music* Box and again featur-
ing a piano. This time the piano is being
transported on a rope bridge across an

"Why must they have pianos on top of the Alps!"

Stan LAUREL SWISS MISS Oliver HARDY

A Metro-Goldwyn-Mayer PICTURE

ABOVE: *In both* THE MUSIC BOX *and* SWISS MISS, *Stan and Ollie do battle with a piano.*

alpine ravine. Stan is somewhat drunk, Ollie is in a temper, and the job becomes excessively complicated when, halfway across, the boys meet a gorilla going in the opposite direction. (What's a gorilla doing in the Swiss Alps? Silly question.)

Military themes were also exploited. In *Bonnie Scotland* (1935) the boys sign on, by mistake, with a Highland regiment and are promptly posted to India. In *Blockheads* (1938), regarded by modern fans as a classic of traditional Laurel and Hardy, Stan is left on sentry duty in the trenches at the end of the First World War. Twenty years later, he is still there, marching up and down, with, behind him, a mountainous pile of empty baked-beans tins.

Between those two films they made their only Western, *Way Out West* (1937). The comic Western is a tricky genre. Many have been attempted; few have succeeded. *Way Out West* is one of the successes. Among other things, the film is notable for Stan and Ollie's singing and dancing, more here than in any other film, and including the famous duet, 'In the Blue Ridge Mountains of Virginia, On the Trail of the Lonesome Pine'. It was a hit single in England in the 1970s, long after Stan and Babe were dead.

The film is full of good things, and there are no dull moments. Several discriminating critics, including David Robinson, pick *Way Out West* as the best of all Laurel and Hardy features. Significantly, it was one of only two films (the other being its immediate predecessor, *Our Relations*) that were officially described as 'A Stan Laurel Production'. Stan, who had set up his own production company and even produced a few cheap Westerns, was only too well aware that in general the Laurel and Hardy feature films had been too loose in structure. Although he of course played an important part in the

scripting and editing of all Laurel and Hardy films, for these two he had complete control (though no share of the profits). The result was much tighter construction. In *Our Relations,* in which Laurel and Hardy play double roles as their own twin brothers,

there was perhaps too much plot, allowing little time for the long-running lunacy of their best jokes. But in *Way Out West* Stan got the mixture just right.

Presumably, Stan intended to control production of all his own movies in future, just as Chaplin had been doing for years, but things did not work out like that. He was unable to make the sort of deal he wanted with Roach, or with any other company. Babe, who was quite happy with what he was offered, was unhappy that Stan's differ-

---

'I wish he [Stan] would come off his high horse.'
BABE COMMENTS ON STAN'S BREACH WITH ROACH

---

ences with Roach made them both idle. Although he enjoyed the race course more than the film studio, he had to eat too. Press reports of rows between Laurel and Hardy, however, were way out of line. The need for money eventually forced Stan, early in 1938, to sign up again with Roach on Roach's terms, which, most people thought, were not unreasonable.

Stan showed no eagerness to work for Roach. Babe was paired with the comedian Harry Langdon for his next film, while Stan negotiated to make a film – it never came off – for yesterday's man, Mack Sennett. Roach lost patience and fired Stan, who retaliated with a suit for damages. Part of Roach's defence was that Stan had violated the morals clause in his contract. Stan was on his third wife, a high-living lady with a police record, but he was appalled by this suggestion.

Babe had a separate contract with Roach, but Stan hoped that in 1939, when Babe's contract was up for renewal, they could achieve independence for Laurel and Hardy. Their lawyer and agent, Ben Shipman, was trying to find another studio interested in doing a Laurel and Hardy series. An independent producer who was associated with RKO signed them up, together with many of their old associates like Jimmy Finlayson, to make *The Flying Deuces.* It was even more obviously derivative of earlier Laurel and Hardy films (especially *Beau Chumps*) than usual, but it was OK. In its most memorable scene Stan consoles Ollie in a military prison by playing the bed springs like a banjo. The film did well in Europe in the early days of Nazi occupation when good laughs were hard to find, and nobody lost any money. Another effect of the film was to restore relations with Hal Roach. Stan still owed Roach two films, he needed money, Babe was agreeable, so they went to work on the old terms. Unfortunately, the reconciliation was half-hearted and temporary.

WIVES

'When two people reach the place in life where they can no longer share a laugh together, then it is practically impossible to share the same bed and board. Laughter is not a trivial part of married life. To the contrary, it is very important.' STAN ON MARRIAGE

FACING PAGE: *Stan Laurel with his second wife, Ruth, and Oliver Hardy with his second wife, Myrtle, at a dinner dance in 1935.*

As EVERYONE KNOWS, those who live in the peculiar environment of the Hollywood film business are subject to two special complaints, the two 'A's: Alcoholism and Adultery.

Like a lot of alcoholics, Stan's trouble seems to have been that he had a very poor head for the stuff. There were times when it affected his work, but it didn't ruin his career and it didn't ruin his health. On rare occasions, domestic violence threatened, but Stan's partners were mostly bigger than he was and no damage was done. During his

RIGHT: *Hardy shows that his divorce problems have emptied his pockets.*

FAR RIGHT: *Oliver Hardy married Lucille Jones in 1940; they enjoyed a happy marriage until his death in 1957.*

later years, on doctor's orders, he drank very little, if at all.

As for Babe Hardy, he was always inclined to spend rather a long time at the nineteenth hole, but he didn't have a serious *drink* problem. Babe's first marriage, to entertainer Madelyn Saloshin when he was just twenty, soon failed. In 1921, after divorcing Madelyn, he married a beautiful brunette, Myrtle Lee. She was not in the

RIGHT: *While Stan had great trouble getting on with women, Babe managed to enjoy a relatively tranquil private life.*

film business, and for years they seemed to have a very successful marriage. But in 1929 Babe fell for an attractive widow, a Southerner like himself, called Viola Morse. At the same time Babe could not bring himself to break with Myrtle. In such a situation, Stan would have hit the bottle; in this case Myrtle did.

After Babe finally split up with Myrtle for good, he was expected to marry Viola, but he fell for Lucille Jones, a continuity girl on the set of *Flying Deuces.* She was attractive, intelligent and humorous. Babe was showing his age and had gone even fatter in the face. However, he charmed her into marriage in 1940 and they remained devoted to each other until Babe's death seventeen years later.

Stan also found the right woman in the end. He had four wives but one of them he married twice. He was married in all but legal title to Mae Dahlberg for nearly ten years. Immediately Mae departed, Stan married Lois Nielsen. In 1927, while Lois was pregnant with their first child, Stan became involved with Alyce Ardell, a minor film actress. She was his mistress, off and on, for about twelve years. Though kind and gentle, Stan was also irresponsible. He had many shorter-lived affairs.

After a messy divorce from Lois in 1935, Stan married Ruth Rogers, a beautiful blonde widow of twenty-seven whom he had picked up while sailing his yacht off Santa Catalina in 1933. They seem to have been genuinely in love but temperamentally unsuited to each other and there were rows from the first. They were divorced in 1937, but never completely lost contact and married again in 1941.

In between came Stan's short and stormy marriage to Ileana Shuvalova, a Russian 'countess'. Apart from bursting uninvited into song in nightclubs, she would wage domestic war with saucepans and other weapons. Stan, who was being sued at the time by two of his ex-wives, built a high brick wall around his house, named 'Fort Laurel', but it didn't stop newsmen joyfully reporting Ileana's escapades.

LEFT: *Stan liked plenty of activity around him, but his brief and stormy marriage to Ileana Shuvalova brought too much conflict.*

'It all interfered with my work … Her conduct caused unfavourable publicity and she mixed with people I didn't care for her to associate with.'
STAN ON DIVORCE FROM ILEANA (1939)

ABOVE: *Ollie and Stan with his wife, Ida, picking up their ration cards during their visit to London in 1947.*

After his second divorce from Ruth, in 1946, Stan married Ida Kitaeva Raphael. She was, like Ileana, a brassy-looking Russian singer and an extrovert personality. Her announcement to the press after their wedding 'No more divorces for Stan Laurel', was greeted with irony, but she was right. She made Stan's last twenty years, when their material circumstances were modest (though not, as some say, poor), perhaps the happiest, certainly the most peaceful, time of his life.

RIGHT: *Stan Laurel with his daughter, Lois.*

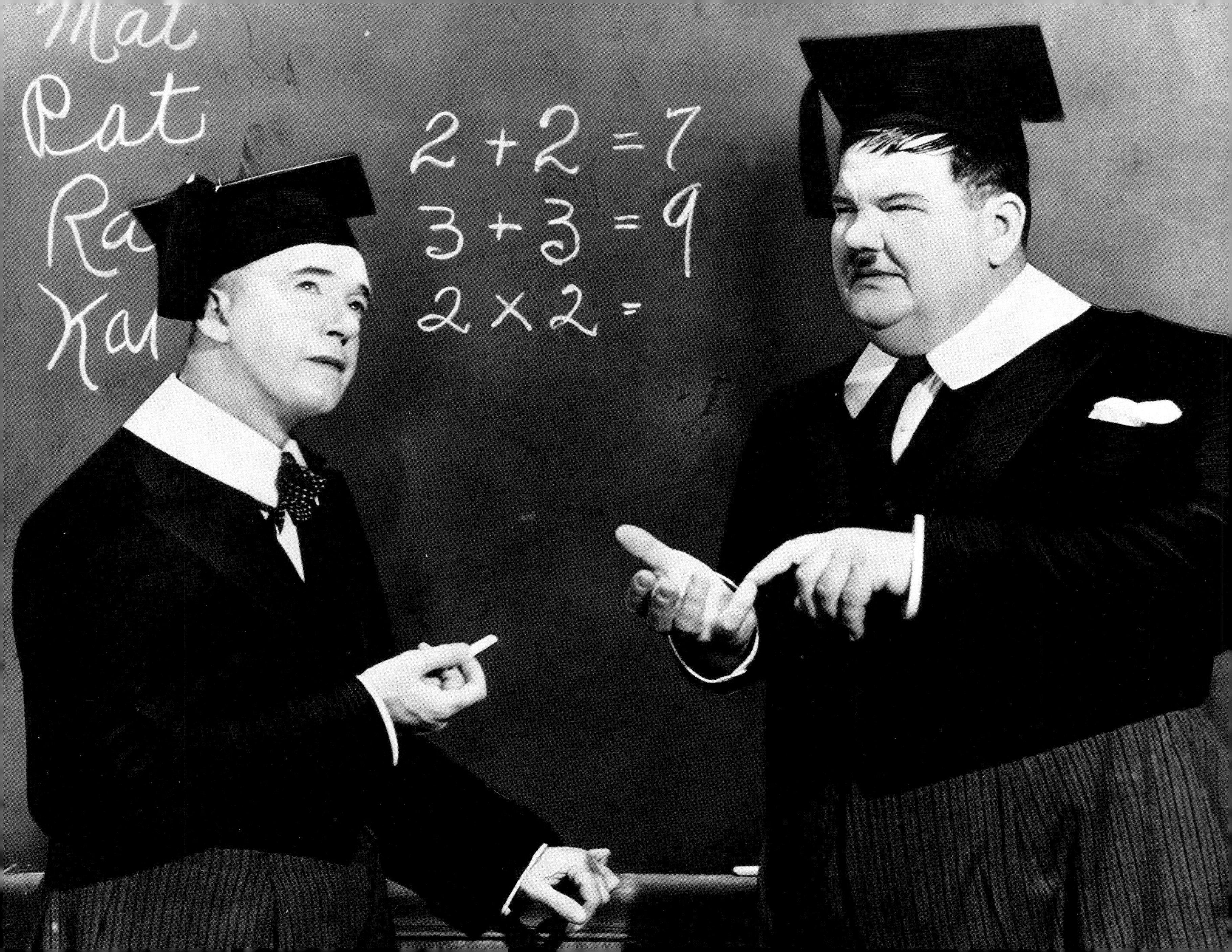
Rat
2 + 2 = 7
3 + 3 = 9
2 × 2 =

LAST FILMS

'Well, here we are at last. Right down in the dust. I wonder what's the matter with us. We're just as good as other people, yet we don't seem to advance ourselves. We never get any place.'
OLLIE'S COMPLAINT (FROM *A CHUMP AT OXFORD*)

'Stan and I have had a lot of fun appearing before you. Thank you, goodbye — and GOD BLESS!'
OLLIE'S LAST CURTAIN CALL (1952)

FACING PAGE: *A CHUMP AT OXFORD was one of Laurel and Hardy's funniest features.*

A *CHUMP AT OXFORD* (the title echoed the recent *A Yank at Oxford*) was unusual in that it partly forsook the usual Stan and Ollie personas. Stan, after a bump on the head, reverts to being Lord Paddington, a great brain, aesthete and sportsman, who is called in to help Professor Einstein sort out his theory of relativity. He does not know Ollie at first ('Who is this coarse person with the foreign accent?') but later hires him as his valet. Apart from the revelation of Stan's acting, it's one of their funniest features: it was Hal Roach's favourite.

BELOW: *Many of Stan's tricks, like flicking a light from his thumb, were later borrowed by other comedians.*

> *'He's got a jolly old face, you know. Breaks the monotony and helps fill up the room.'*
> STAN ON OLLIE (FROM *A CHUMP AT OXFORD*)

They made one more film for Roach, *Saps at Sea*, very watchable though not in the same class as *A Chump at Oxford*. There was no script when production started; Stan and his colleagues made it up day by day.

Their last film for Roach was not the end of their film career, but in some ways they might have been happier if it had been. Other studios were not exactly lining up to sign them on, but eventually Darryl Zanuck's Fox studio did. The boys needed the money, otherwise they would not have taken the deal they were offered. Stan no longer had any artistic control. Their films were intended to fill the bill as the 'supporting feature'.

The first one, *Great Guns* (1941), had some fine moments, such as Stan, in need of a shaving light, screwing a light bulb into his mouth. This and many more of Stan's tricks, like flicking a light from his thumb in Way Out West, were to be 'borrowed' by

FACING PAGE: *In 1945, Laurel and Hardy made* NOTHING BUT TROUBLE *for MGM.*

'I've had so many nice things happen to me … it's sort of hard to sort out. But I guess you'd call my best moment this one. When I was a boy, my mother would occasionally go to fortune-tellers and one day she went to visit a lady in Decatur, Georgia. This lady told Mama that one day her son's name would be known all over the world. It's nice to know that she saw that prophecy come true.' BABE'S VIEW OF FAME

other comedians and by makers of television commercials.

In the next three years they made five more films for Fox, plus two on loan to MGM. The Fox material was summed up by Fred Guiles, Stan's best biographer, as 'awful tripe'. For all his faults, Stan was never a man to hold a grudge for long, but he remained bitter about their treatment at Fox until the end of his days. In 1945 the boys were so fed up that they asked to be released from their contract. The studio made no objection.

Stan and Babe were still hugely popular, as was shown by their personal appearances. In 1947 the British impresario Bernard Delfont booked them into the London Palladium and major provincial centres. Large crowds were waiting to greet them at Waterloo station in London. At the end of the English tour, they moved on to Paris, the Low Countries and Sweden before returning to semi-retirement in Los Angeles.

Television brought them a new generation of admirers. They were deluged with fan mail, more than they had received at the height of their film career. Stan tried to answer every letter individually, but the sheer weight of his mailbag overcame him.

LEFT: *On board the* QUEEN ELIZABETH *at Southampton in 1947, arriving for their tour of Britain and Europe.*

Five years after they had bowed out from the Fox studio, an offer came to make a film in France. They set off for Paris, where they found an unwritten script, a hopelessly inefficient production company, and a daft director – not to mention a formidable language barrier. Filming was supposed to last twelve weeks but took a year. The film is variously known as *Atoll K, Utopia* and *Robinson Crusoeland*. Stan fell ill during filming, and he certainly looks it. Babe also became ill, the first signs of heart trouble.

They both recovered sufficiently to make another English tour in 1952. Stan had written a new sketch, *Birds of a Feather,* in which the third character is, for once, not a beleaguered policeman but a mad psychiatrist, Dr Berserk. Delfont persuaded them to return again the following year, but they had made their last tour.

Back home, there were plans to make a series of children's films, *The Fables of Laurel and Hardy* for Hal Roach Jr, with Stan in full control. These plans were scotched when Babe had a serious heart attack in 1954. It was his second, and the doctors insisted on his losing weight. He lost 68 kg (150 pounds) in a few months, becoming a mere sack of a man. Soon afterwards Stan had a stroke, which affected his mind as well as his

RIGHT: *Atoll K had only a limited release – much to Stan and Babe's relief.*

'*Joannon [the director] is funnier than the picture, although* THAT'*s not saying a hell of a lot ...*'
STAN ON THE MAKING OF *ATOLL K*

'With pleasure I am sending you herewith another photograph … Sorry that Mr Hardy is unable to sign it on account of his illness — speech is affected (unable to talk). Poor fellow is in bad shape and still confined to bed (7 months now), it's certainly distressing. I too had a slight stroke two years ago … but fortunately I made a wonderful recovery — thank God — and am able to get around quite well again. However, I doubt if I shall ever be in shape to work again …'

LETTER TO A FAN (1957)

movements. He was to make a complete recovery, but, though Stan still nourished hopes of Babe being restored to the Ollie of old, it was the end for Laurel and Hardy.

Babe suffered a third heart attack at Christmas 1955. It would have been best if he had died then, for there were serious complications. For the last year of his life he was a hopeless invalid, unable to speak and understanding little, but lovingly tended at home by Lucille.

ABOVE LEFT: *Laurel and Hardy were entrusted with opening a new section of railway to the public on their 1947 English tour.*

BELOW LEFT: *Stan and Babe on stage during their final English tour in 1952.*

Babe died on 7 August 1957. Stan, in poor health anyway, could not bring himself to go to the funeral.

As an old man, Stan's health seems to have improved a little, and he enjoyed a tranquil retirement guarded, ferociously if necessary, against unwanted intrusions by the devoted Ida. His chief enjoyment was talking of old times – often with old Roach hands like Joe Finck, a filmcutter, or old vaudeville pals – and basking in the admiration of people like Jerry Lewis, who liked to run over his material with Stan, and Marcel Marceau, whose career Stan had helped when the young mime was almost unknown, describing him at a press conference in France as an 'unsung genius'. In return, the great French mime said of him, 'Stan Laurel is a *maître*. He is of the mime that goes back to the very oldest days of the juggler and the comic troubadour.'

In February 1965 Stan had another stroke, and by 23 February it became clear that he would not recover. As he lay in bed, he beckoned to a nurse. 'I'd rather be skiing than doing this,' he murmured.

'Do you ski, Mr Laurel?' said the nurse.

'No,' said Stan, 'but I'd rather be doing that than this.'

A few minutes later he was dead.

'How I wish I could answer them all with a big, long letter. But there's just no way to do that. I deeply appreciate it, but it's physically impossible. The people who write are so damned nice, you feel obligated. Many of them want to become pen pals, and I write saying I'd like to hear from them occasionally. However, I do write consistently to collectors of Laurel and Hardy films because I have an obligation to them.'
STAN'S RESPONSE TO FANS (C. 1961)

'If anyone at my funeral has a long face, I'll never speak to him again.' STAN ON FUNERALS

LAUREL & HARDY FILMOGRAPHY

This list includes only official Laurel & Hardy releases.

F = feature.

Others are two reels unless otherwise specified.

1927
Putting Pants on Philip
The Second Hundred Years
Hats Off
The Battle of the Century

(Laurel and Hardy appeared in several 1927 'Comedy All Stars' shorts, made by Roach and distributed by Pathé)

1928
Leave 'Em Laughing
Flying Elephants
The Finishing Touch
From Soup to Nuts
You're Darn Tootin'
Their Purple Moment
Should Married Men Go Home
Early to Bed
Two Tars
Habeas Corpus
We Faw Down

1929
Liberty
Wrong Again
That's My Wife
Big Business
Double Whoopee
Berth Marks
Men O' War
Bacon Grabbers
Angora Love
Unaccustomed As We Are
The Perfect Day
They Go Boom
The Hoosegow

1930
Night Owls
Blotto
Brats
The Laurence and Hardy
   Murder Mystery (3 reels)
Below Zero
Hog Wild
Another Fine Mess (3 reels)

1931
Be Big (3 reels)
Chickens Come Home (3 reels)
Laughing Gravy
Our Wife
Come Clean
One Good Turn

Pardon Us (F)
Beau Chumps (Beau Hunks)
(4 reels)

1932
Helpmates
Any Old Port
The Music Box (3 reels)
The Chimp (3 reels)
County Hospital
Scram!
Pack Up Your Troubles (F)
Their First Mistake
Towed in a Hole

1933
Twice Two
Me and My Pal
The Devil's Brother (Fra
   Diavolo) (F)
The Midnight Patrol
Busy Bodies
Dirty Work
Sons of the Desert (F)

1934
Oliver the Eighth
Going Bye-Bye
Them Thar Hills
Babes in Toyland (F)
The Live Ghost

1935
Tit for Tat
The Fixer Uppers
Thicker Than Water
Bonnie Scotland (F)

1936
The Bohemian Girl (F)
Our Relations (F)

1937
Way Out West (F)
Pick a Star (F)

1938
Swiss Miss (F)
Blockheads (F)

1939
The Flying Deuces (F)

1940
A Chump at Oxford (F)
Saps at Sea (F)

1941
Great Guns (F, for Fox)

1942
A-Haunting We Will Go
   (F, for Fox)

1943
Air Raid Wardens (F, for
   MGM)
Jitterbugs (F, for Fox)
The Dancing Masters (F, for
   Fox)

1944
The Big Noise (F, for Fox)

1945
The Bullfighters (F, for Fox)
Nothing But Trouble
   (F, for MGM)

1950
Atoll K (F, Les Films Sirius)